MANIFEST LIKE A MOTHERF*CKER

A No-Bullsh*t Guide to Getting What You Want

Quarto

This edition published in 2026 by Chartwell Books,
an imprint of The Quarto Group
142 West 36th Street, 4th Floor
New York, NY 10018 USA
T (212) 779-4972
www.Quarto.com

Contains content originally published as *Manifest Your Intentions* in 2022 by Chartwell Books.

10 9 8 7 6 5 4 3 2 1

Chartwell titles are also available at discount for retail, wholesale, promotional, and bulk purchase. For details, contact the Special Sales Manager by email at specialsales@quarto.com or by mail at The Quarto Group, Attn: Special Sales Manager, 100 Cummings Center Suite 265D, Beverly, MA 01915, USA.

ISBN: 978-0-7858-4906-3

Publisher: Wendy Friedman
Publishing Director: Meredith Mennitt
Cover Designer: Brianna Tong
Interior Designer: Kate Sinclair

Printed in Malaysia

EEA Representation, WTS Tax d.o.o.,
Žanova ulica 3, 4000 Kranj, Slovenia.
www.wts-tax.si

Manifesting the Life of Your Dreams

By picking up this book, you are already on your way to changing your life and welcoming a brighter future.

Manifestation is the practice of turn your dreams into reality. You focus on specific aspirational goals with the purpose of making them real. This is sometimes called "setting intentions" and while it is becoming increasingly popular, it has been around for hundreds of years. *The Upanishads*, ancient Sanskrit texts contained in the *Vedas*, tell us, "You are what your deepest desire is. As your desire is, so is your intention. As your intention is, so is your will. As your will is, so is your deed. As your deed is, so is your destiny."

Manifestation relies on the "Law of Attraction." This philosophy suggests that positive thoughts and actions bring forth positive results. Likewise, negativity attracts more negativity. So, it is important that when you set your intentions or create a manifestation statement, that you go into it with an open, positive heart and mind.

EXAMPLES OF INTENTIONS OR MANIFESTATION STATEMENTS

At its core, manifestation is about identifying what you want to bring into your life and creating that outcome. It is deeply personal and you should note that you are only able to manifest your own intentions. Creating a specific manifestation statement helps us focus our subconscious and visualize that reality. Therefore, the most successful intentions begin with "I am" or "I will" or "I intend."

It is also important to write these statements using the present or past tense rather than the future tense. It doesn't matter which one of these two tenses you use; some people like to write as if they're in the future looking back on what they've achieved, while others like to write as if they're actually in the middle of living out their manifestations. Both work perfectly fine. What you need to avoid is using the future tense.

Also, remember that you can only manifest realities for your own life—you can't manifest on behalf of other people.

Why Use a Manifestation Journal?

As mentioned earlier, manifestation focuses on transforming thoughts into reality. The act of writing brings your thoughts into the physical realm. It connects your mind to your body. This seemingly small act amplifies the energy you are putting into your future dreams and goals.

Additionally, keeping a manifestation journal provides structure and maintain motivation. Shifting your mindset, perspective, and opening your heart to new possibilities takes consistency. The daily and weekly exercises in this book will help you stay on track while stoking your creativity.

How to Use this Book

This book is designed as a 100-day manifestation journey. It is divided into 13 weeks, covering 100 days. It is not dated or linked to a specific part of the calendar year, so you can begin anytime. While it's recommended write daily for maximum effectiveness, if you miss a day, you can easily pick up where you left off.

We will cover a variety of manifestation exercises and techniques. After completing this journal, you will know which techniques proved most successful for you and will be able to personalize your future manifestation practice. But for now, try to keep an open mind and give each exercise a try.

WEEKLY OVERVIEW

This workbook begins with a weekly overview. Before completing it, focus on your week ahead. What do you want to manifest this week? Write down tangible action items that will help manifest that intention. Manifestation begins in the mind, but we must meet the Universe halfway and support our desired intentions through positive and progressive actions.

Throughout the week, refer back to this page to stay focused and use the Tracker to record your activity.

WEEK # 1

Manifestation Statement for the Week

Action Plan

1.
2.
3.
4.
5.

✱	mon.	tues.	wed.	thu.	fri.	sat.	sun.
Daily Journaling							
Affirmations							
Gratitude							
369 Exercise							

16

DAILY PAGES

There are 100 daily journaling pages that will help you keep your intentions front of mind. Depending on the time of day you check in to your journal, the visualization exercise will help you project and anticipate a successful day or, if you are writing in the evening, allow you to reflect on the day's wins and rewrite the script of any challenges you encountered.

Additionally, you can develop a daily gratitude practice. It is important to take time to acknowledge and be thankful for all the wonderful things that you currently have in your life if you wish to invite more joy and success in the future.

DAY # 5 / /

What is your intention-setting focus today?

I am grateful for...

I am grateful for...

I am grateful for...

I am grateful for...

I am grateful for...

HOW DO YOU WANT TO FEEL TODAY?

IF YOU ARE JOURNALING IN THE MORNING, visualize your day going successfully and describe it here. **IF YOU ARE WRITING AT THE END OF THE DAY,** reflect on how the day went and write out how you would rescript any parts to be more successful.

26

369 METHOD

The 369 method is a manifestation exercise. Many people, including renowned physicist and inventor Nicola Tesla, believe that the numbers 3, 6, and 9 hold great significance in the workings of the Universe.

The 369 method is simple: using the 369 Method worksheets, you will write down what you're trying to manifest three times as soon as you wake up in the morning. Then, in the afternoon, write your manifestation statement six times. Finally, in the evening before bed write it nine times. The repeated consistency, frequency and intention will start to take root within you and, over time, you will begin to embody and attract your manifestation.

Try to do the 369 method exercise three times a week (or more if it resonates with you!)

369 *Method*

Write your manifestation statement 3 times when you first wake up.

MORNING

1.
2.
3.

Take time during your day to write your manifestation statement 6 times.

DAY

1.
2.
3.
4.
5.
6.

Before you go to bed, write out your manifestation statement 9 times.

NIGHT

1.
2.
3.
4.
5.
6.
7.
8.
9.

17

The Power of Positive Affirmations

A positive affirmation, or mantra, is a statement of belief or attitude that you want to internalize and manifest. They are used in manifestation to change your generalized attitudes about yourself and your life. They are usually not as specific as manifestation or intention setting statements.

Affirmations are written in the present tense to make us believe that the goal is already achieved, or attitude adopted. They are written or spoken repeatedly until our minds accept them as truth. When our mind accepts the affirmation, the manifestation follows. Affirmations can also be used to overcome negative thoughts and self-sabotaging beliefs. They can also be used to boost our confidence and attract more positivity.

On the following pages there are examples of helpful positive affirmations that relate to different areas of your life. For each category, circle the ones that resonate with you.

Additionally, at the end of this book, there are little positive affirmations cards. Cut out and slip these into your wallet or pass a sweet note to a friend who needs a reminder of their greatness.

CONFIDENCE AND SELF-ESTEEM

I am strong and confident.

I am worthy of what I desire.

I am adventurous.

I am brave and have overcome my fears.

I am in control of my life.

I am awesome.

I am the hero of my own life.

I can. I will.

I enjoy meeting new people.

Write additional positive affirmations relating to
CONFIDENCE AND SELF-ESTEEM

PHYSICAL HEALTH AND BODY IMAGE

I love my body.

My body is allowed to change.

I am so much more than my appearance.

I feel joyful in my body.

I trust in my body's ability to heal.

I am making today count.

It's my time.

I accept myself how I am and embrace self-love.

I will not compare myself to others.

My body is a gift.

Write additional positive affirmations relating to
PHYSICAL HEALTH AND BODY IMAGE

MONEY AND FINANCIAL ABUNDANCE

I always have enough money.

My financial situation is improving.

I am worthy of having money.

I am wealthy beyond money.

I trust myself to make sound financial decisions.

I have profitable skills.

I accept financial success.

My life is rich and full.

I am allowed to have success and happiness.

I am happy and grateful that I am now earning a robust salary.

Write additional positive affirmations relating to
MONEY AND FINANCIAL ABUNDANCE

WORK AND CAREER

I believe in my skills and talents.

My skill set is impressive.

I am creating a work life that motivates and inspires me.

Being successful at work is easy for me.

I am driven towards success.

I always achieve my work goals.

I make smart moves and decisions.

I let go of my work-related stress.

Success and wealth come easily to me.

I know I will find my dream job.

Write additional positive affirmations relating to
WORK AND CAREER

LOVE AND RELATIONSHIPS

I am open to give and receive love.

I believe in love.

I am ready to meet my soulmate.

Others treasure my love.

I am attracting a kind, loving partner.

I choose love not fear.

The love I am seeking is seeking me.

I am choosing and not waiting to be chosen.

I am worthy of love.

I am radiating love.

Write additional positive affirmations relating to
LOVE AND RELATIONSHIPS

Manifestation Statement for the Week

Action Plan

1.
2.
3.
4.
5.

✷	mon.	tues.	wed.	thu.	fri.	sat.	sun.
Daily Journaling							
Affirmations							
Gratitude							
369 Exercise							

Write your manifestation statement 3 times when you first wake up.

MORNING

1.
2.
3.

Take time during your day to write your manifestation statement 6 times.

DAY

1.
2.
3.
4.
5.
6.

Before you go to bed, write out your manifestation statement 9 times.

NIGHT

1.
2.
3.
4.
5.
6.
7.
8.
9.

MORNING

1.

2.

3.

DAY

1.

2.

3.

4.

5.

6.

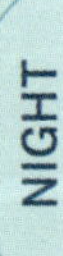

NIGHT

1.

2.

3.

4.

5.

6.

7.

8.

9.

MORNING

1.
2.
3.

DAY

1.
2.
3.
4.
5.
6.

NIGHT

1.
2.
3.
4.
5.
6.
7.
8.
9.

Get Specific!

Visualization is an important manifestation exercise. It calls upon the law of attractions and awakens your creative subconscious to recognize opportunities that might have otherwise ignored. But the key is to be as specific as you can when envisioning what you wish to manifest.

DESCRIBE WHAT YOU WANT TO MANIFEST USING SPECIFIC SENSORY DETAILS. A new house? What are you planting in that backyard garden? What color are the kitchen walls? *Dive deep!*

DAY # 1 / /

What is your intention-setting focus today?

I am grateful for...

I am grateful for...

I am grateful for...

I am grateful for...

I am grateful for...

HOW DO YOU WANT TO FEEL TODAY?

IF YOU ARE JOURNALING IN THE MORNING, visualize your day going successfully and describe it here. **IF YOU ARE WRITING AT THE END OF THE DAY,** reflect on how the day went and write out how you would rescript any parts to be more successful.

DAY # 2 / /

What is your intention-setting focus today?

I am grateful for...

I am grateful for...

I am grateful for...

I am grateful for...

I am grateful for...

HOW DO YOU WANT TO FEEL TODAY?

IF YOU ARE JOURNALING IN THE MORNING, visualize your day going successfully and describe it here. **IF YOU ARE WRITING AT THE END OF THE DAY,** reflect on how the day went and write out how you would rescript any parts to be more successful.

DAY # 3 / /

What is your intention-setting focus today?

I am grateful for...

I am grateful for...

I am grateful for...

I am grateful for...

I am grateful for...

HOW DO YOU WANT TO FEEL TODAY?

IF YOU ARE JOURNALING IN THE MORNING, visualize your day going successfully and describe it here. **IF YOU ARE WRITING AT THE END OF THE DAY,** reflect on how the day went and write out how you would rescript any parts to be more successful.

DAY # 4 / /

What is your intention-setting focus today?

I am grateful for...

I am grateful for...

I am grateful for...

I am grateful for...

I am grateful for...

HOW DO YOU WANT TO FEEL TODAY?

IF YOU ARE JOURNALING IN THE MORNING, visualize your day going successfully and describe it here. **IF YOU ARE WRITING AT THE END OF THE DAY,** reflect on how the day went and write out how you would rescript any parts to be more successful.

DAY # 5 / /

What is your intention-setting focus today?

I am grateful for...

I am grateful for...

I am grateful for...

I am grateful for...

I am grateful for...

HOW DO YOU WANT TO FEEL TODAY?

IF YOU ARE JOURNALING IN THE MORNING, visualize your day going successfully and describe it here. **IF YOU ARE WRITING AT THE END OF THE DAY,** reflect on how the day went and write out how you would rescript any parts to be more successful.

DAY # 6 / /

What is your intention-setting focus today?

I am grateful for...

I am grateful for...

I am grateful for...

I am grateful for...

I am grateful for...

HOW DO YOU WANT TO FEEL TODAY?

IF YOU ARE JOURNALING IN THE MORNING, visualize your day going successfully and describe it here. **IF YOU ARE WRITING AT THE END OF THE DAY,** reflect on how the day went and write out how you would rescript any parts to be more successful.

DAY # 7 / /

What is your intention-setting focus today?

I am grateful for...

I am grateful for...

I am grateful for...

I am grateful for...

I am grateful for...

HOW DO YOU WANT TO FEEL TODAY?

IF YOU ARE JOURNALING IN THE MORNING, visualize your day going successfully and describe it here. **IF YOU ARE WRITING AT THE END OF THE DAY,** reflect on how the day went and write out how you would rescript any parts to be more successful.

DAY # 8 / /

What is your intention-setting focus today?

I am grateful for...

I am grateful for...

I am grateful for...

I am grateful for...

I am grateful for...

HOW DO YOU WANT TO FEEL TODAY?

IF YOU ARE JOURNALING IN THE MORNING, visualize your day going successfully and describe it here. **IF YOU ARE WRITING AT THE END OF THE DAY,** reflect on how the day went and write out how you would rescript any parts to be more successful.

Manifestation Statement for the Week

Action Plan

1. ____
2. ____
3. ____
4. ____
5. ____

	mon.	tues.	wed.	thu.	fri.	sat.	sun.
Daily Journaling							
Affirmations							
Gratitude							
369 Exercise							

Write your manifestation statement 3 times when you first wake up.

MORNING

1. ______________________________
2. ______________________________
3. ______________________________

Take time during your day to write your manifestation statement 6 times.

DAY

1. ______________________________
2. ______________________________
3. ______________________________
4. ______________________________
5. ______________________________
6. ______________________________

Before you go to bed, write out your manifestation statement 9 times.

NIGHT

1. ______________________________
2. ______________________________
3. ______________________________
4. ______________________________
5. ______________________________
6. ______________________________
7. ______________________________
8. ______________________________
9. ______________________________

MORNING

1.
2.
3.

DAY

1.
2.
3.
4.
5.
6.

NIGHT

1.
2.
3.
4.
5.
6.
7.
8.
9.

MORNING

1.
2.
3.

DAY

1.
2.
3.
4.
5.
6.

NIGHT

1.
2.
3.
4.
5.
6.
7.
8.
9.

It's time to pump yourself up and acknowledge all the wins you've had so far.

CREATE A LIST OF SOME OF THE AMAZING THINGS YOU'VE ACCOMPLISHED IN LIFE. This may seem hard at first because we rarely give ourselves credit for all the incredible things we do. There might be some easy, big victories to spot (write them down!) but be sure to look for the *small victories that are so often overlooked but need to be celebrated.*

DAY # 9 / /

What is your intention-setting focus today?

I am grateful for...

I am grateful for...

I am grateful for...

I am grateful for...

I am grateful for...

HOW DO YOU WANT TO FEEL TODAY?

IF YOU ARE JOURNALING IN THE MORNING, visualize your day going successfully and describe it here. **IF YOU ARE WRITING AT THE END OF THE DAY,** reflect on how the day went and write out how you would rescript any parts to be more successful.

DAY # 10 / /

What is your intention-setting focus today?

I am grateful for...

I am grateful for...

I am grateful for...

I am grateful for...

I am grateful for...

HOW DO YOU WANT TO FEEL TODAY?

IF YOU ARE JOURNALING IN THE MORNING, visualize your day going successfully and describe it here. **IF YOU ARE WRITING AT THE END OF THE DAY,** reflect on how the day went and write out how you would rescript any parts to be more successful.

DAY # 11   /   /

What is your intention-setting focus today?

I am grateful for...

I am grateful for...

I am grateful for...

I am grateful for...

I am grateful for...

HOW DO YOU WANT TO FEEL TODAY?

IF YOU ARE JOURNALING IN THE MORNING, visualize your day going successfully and describe it here. **IF YOU ARE WRITING AT THE END OF THE DAY,** reflect on how the day went and write out how you would rescript any parts to be more successful.

What is your intention-setting focus today?

I am grateful for...

I am grateful for...

I am grateful for...

I am grateful for...

I am grateful for...

HOW DO YOU WANT TO FEEL TODAY?

IF YOU ARE JOURNALING IN THE MORNING, visualize your day going successfully and describe it here. **IF YOU ARE WRITING AT THE END OF THE DAY,** reflect on how the day went and write out how you would rescript any parts to be more successful.

DAY # 13 / /

What is your intention-setting focus today?

I am grateful for...

I am grateful for...

I am grateful for...

I am grateful for...

I am grateful for...

HOW DO YOU WANT TO FEEL TODAY?

IF YOU ARE JOURNALING IN THE MORNING, visualize your day going successfully and describe it here. **IF YOU ARE WRITING AT THE END OF THE DAY,** reflect on how the day went and write out how you would rescript any parts to be more successful.

DAY # 14 / /

What is your intention-setting focus today?

I am grateful for...

I am grateful for...

I am grateful for...

I am grateful for...

I am grateful for...

HOW DO YOU WANT TO FEEL TODAY?

IF YOU ARE JOURNALING IN THE MORNING, visualize your day going successfully and describe it here. **IF YOU ARE WRITING AT THE END OF THE DAY,** reflect on how the day went and write out how you would rescript any parts to be more successful.

DAY # 15 / /

What is your intention-setting focus today?

I am grateful for...

I am grateful for...

I am grateful for...

I am grateful for...

I am grateful for...

HOW DO YOU WANT TO FEEL TODAY?

IF YOU ARE JOURNALING IN THE MORNING, visualize your day going successfully and describe it here. **IF YOU ARE WRITING AT THE END OF THE DAY,** reflect on how the day went and write out how you would rescript any parts to be more successful.

What is your intention-setting focus today?

I am grateful for...

I am grateful for...

I am grateful for...

I am grateful for...

I am grateful for...

HOW DO YOU WANT TO FEEL TODAY?

IF YOU ARE JOURNALING IN THE MORNING, visualize your day going successfully and describe it here. **IF YOU ARE WRITING AT THE END OF THE DAY,** reflect on how the day went and write out how you would rescript any parts to be more successful.

Manifestation Statement for the Week

Action Plan

1.
2.
3.
4.
5.

✷	mon.	tues.	wed.	thu.	fri.	sat.	sun.
Daily Journaling							
Affirmations							
Gratitude							
369 Exercise							

369 *Method*

Write your manifestation statement 3 times when you first wake up.

MORNING

1.
2.
3.

Take time during your day to write your manifestation statement 6 times.

DAY

1.
2.
3.
4.
5.
6.

Before you go to bed, write out your manifestation statement 9 times.

NIGHT

1.
2.
3.
4.
5.
6.
7.
8.
9.

369 *Method*

MORNING

1.

2.

3.

DAY

1.

2.

3.

4.

5.

6.

NIGHT

1.

2.

3.

4.

5.

6.

7.

8.

9.

MORNING

1.
2.
3.

DAY

1.
2.
3.
4.
5.
6.

NIGHT

1.
2.
3.
4.
5.
6.
7.
8.
9.

Vision Boards

Another tool in your manifestation toolbox is a vision board. A vision board is a physical space to collect images, quotes, drawings that inspire and help you visualize what you want to attract and manifest into your life.

Like other visualization techniques, try to be specific about your vision. Also make sure that everything on your vision board is something you want. Do not put anything you do not want on the board. For example, if a goal is quitting smoking, do not put an image of a cigarette (even with a line through it, or crossed out, or crushed) on the board.

Collect images from magazines, the internet, old photos. You can paste images you've collected on the following pages or you can use a bulletin board.

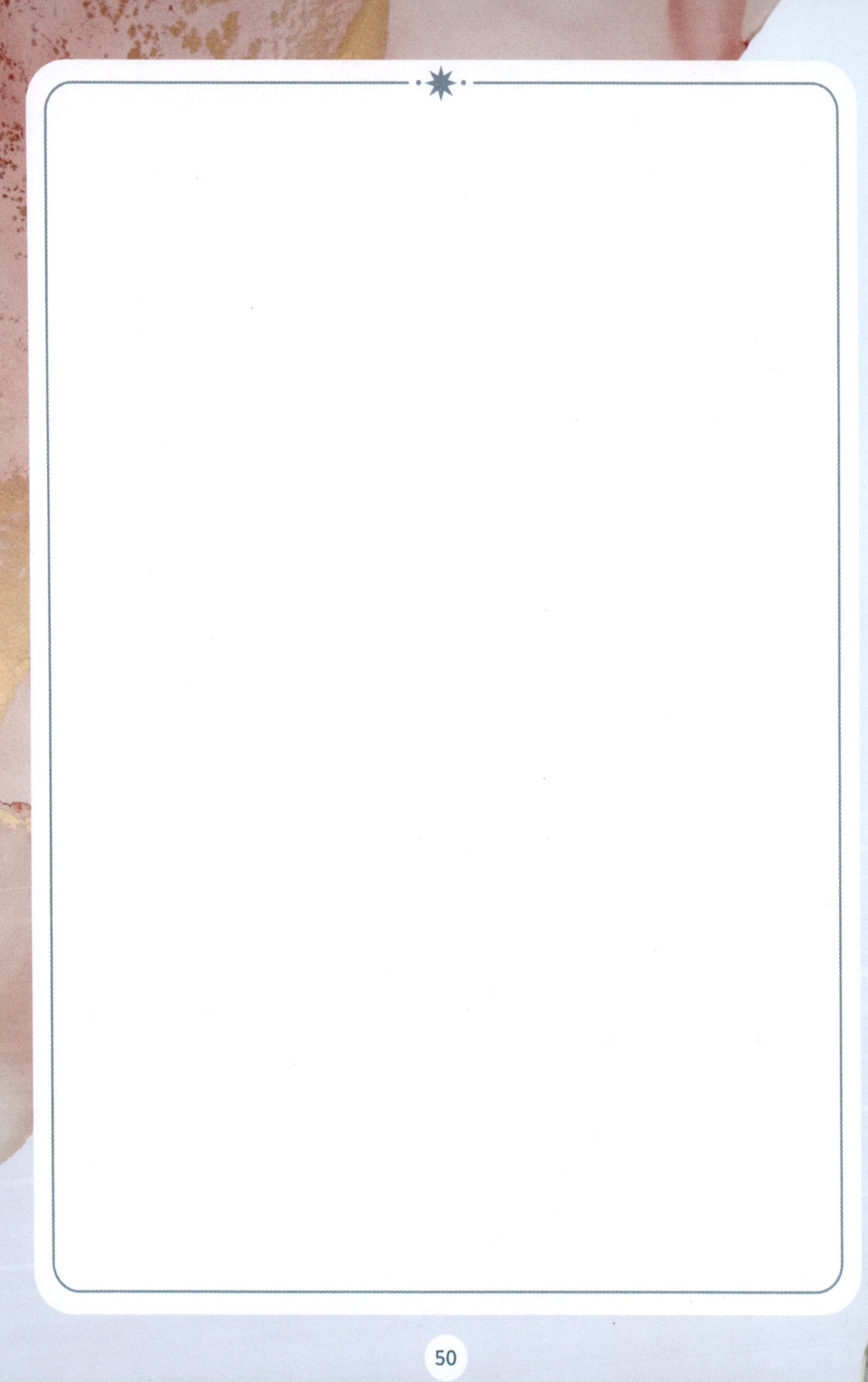

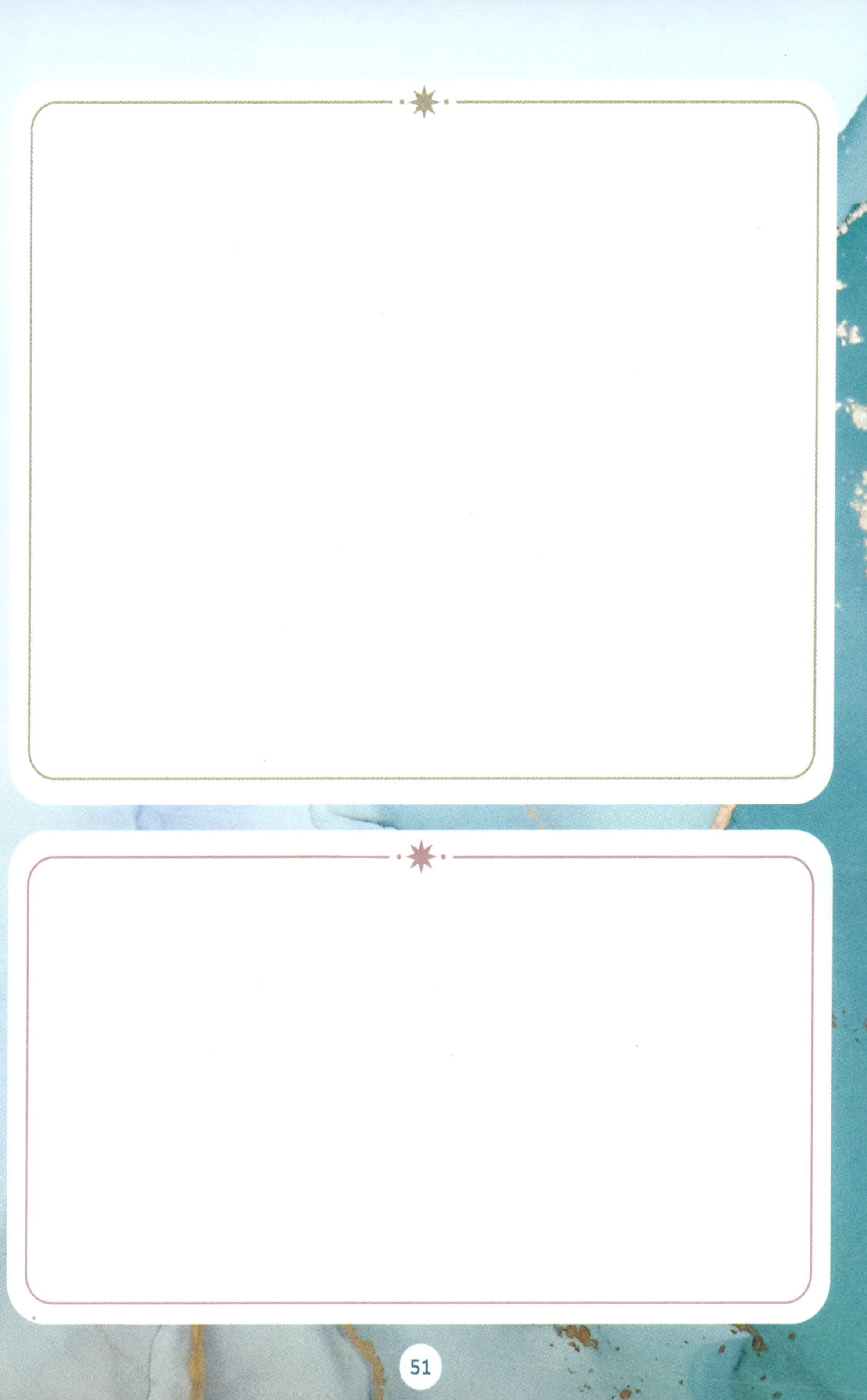

What is your intention-setting focus today?

I am grateful for...

I am grateful for...

I am grateful for...

I am grateful for...

I am grateful for...

HOW DO YOU WANT TO FEEL TODAY?

IF YOU ARE JOURNALING IN THE MORNING, visualize your day going successfully and describe it here. **IF YOU ARE WRITING AT THE END OF THE DAY,** reflect on how the day went and write out how you would rescript any parts to be more successful.

What is your intention-setting focus today?

I am grateful for...

I am grateful for...

I am grateful for...

I am grateful for...

I am grateful for...

HOW DO YOU WANT TO FEEL TODAY?

IF YOU ARE JOURNALING IN THE MORNING, visualize your day going successfully and describe it here. **IF YOU ARE WRITING AT THE END OF THE DAY,** reflect on how the day went and write out how you would rescript any parts to be more successful.

What is your intention-setting focus today?

I am grateful for...

I am grateful for...

I am grateful for...

I am grateful for...

I am grateful for...

HOW DO YOU WANT TO FEEL TODAY?

IF YOU ARE JOURNALING IN THE MORNING, visualize your day going successfully and describe it here. **IF YOU ARE WRITING AT THE END OF THE DAY,** reflect on how the day went and write out how you would rescript any parts to be more successful.

DAY # 20 / /

What is your intention-setting focus today?

I am grateful for...

I am grateful for...

I am grateful for...

I am grateful for...

I am grateful for...

HOW DO YOU WANT TO FEEL TODAY?

IF YOU ARE JOURNALING IN THE MORNING, visualize your day going successfully and describe it here. **IF YOU ARE WRITING AT THE END OF THE DAY,** reflect on how the day went and write out how you would rescript any parts to be more successful.

DAY # 21 / /

What is your intention-setting focus today?

I am grateful for...

I am grateful for...

I am grateful for...

I am grateful for...

I am grateful for...

HOW DO YOU WANT TO FEEL TODAY?

IF YOU ARE JOURNALING IN THE MORNING, visualize your day going successfully and describe it here. **IF YOU ARE WRITING AT THE END OF THE DAY,** reflect on how the day went and write out how you would rescript any parts to be more successful.

DAY # 22 / /

What is your intention-setting focus today?

I am grateful for...

I am grateful for...

I am grateful for...

I am grateful for...

I am grateful for...

HOW DO YOU WANT TO FEEL TODAY?

IF YOU ARE JOURNALING IN THE MORNING, visualize your day going successfully and describe it here. **IF YOU ARE WRITING AT THE END OF THE DAY,** reflect on how the day went and write out how you would rescript any parts to be more successful.

DAY # 23 / /

What is your intention-setting focus today?

I am grateful for...

I am grateful for...

I am grateful for...

I am grateful for...

I am grateful for...

HOW DO YOU WANT TO FEEL TODAY?

IF YOU ARE JOURNALING IN THE MORNING, visualize your day going successfully and describe it here. **IF YOU ARE WRITING AT THE END OF THE DAY,** reflect on how the day went and write out how you would rescript any parts to be more successful.

DAY # 24 / /

What is your intention-setting focus today?

I am grateful for...

I am grateful for...

I am grateful for...

I am grateful for...

I am grateful for...

HOW DO YOU WANT TO FEEL TODAY?

IF YOU ARE JOURNALING IN THE MORNING, visualize your day going successfully and describe it here. **IF YOU ARE WRITING AT THE END OF THE DAY,** reflect on how the day went and write out how you would rescript any parts to be more successful.

Manifestation Statement for the Week

Action Plan

1.
2.
3.
4.
5.

✸	mon.	tues.	wed.	thu.	fri.	sat.	sun.
Daily Journaling							
Affirmations							
Gratitude							
369 Exercise							

Write your manifestation statement 3 times when you first wake up.

1.
2.
3.

MORNING

Take time during your day to write your manifestation statement 6 times.

1.
2.
3.
4.
5.
6.

DAY

Before you go to bed, write out your manifestation statement 9 times.

1.
2.
3.
4.
5.
6.
7.
8.
9.

NIGHT

MORNING

1.
2.
3.

DAY

1.
2.
3.
4.
5.
6.

NIGHT

1.
2.
3.
4.
5.
6.
7.
8.
9.

MORNING

1.
2.
3.

DAY

1.
2.
3.
4.
5.
6.

NIGHT

1.
2.
3.
4.
5.
6.
7.
8.
9.

The Power of the Moon

The moon is both steadfast and everchanging. Each phase of the moon presents an opportunity to invite its purposeful energy into our life and reflect it back to the Universe in manifesting our goals.

The beginning of the moon's cycle, known as the New Moon, is the most fertile time for planting new ideas and desires and an ideal time to invite the moon's purposeful energy into our life and to aid us in manifesting our intentions.

NEW MOON RITUAL

- Gather index card, pen, coloring tools, scissors, ribbon, or string.
- Write your intention on the card, then decorate if you wish.
- Fold the card in half and create a hole through both sides of the open end, in the center of the length, like a gift tag. Secure an 18-inch (45 cm) length of ribbon through the hole of each card.
- Tie the wishes outside to a tree, bush, railing, or other object, where they can be exposed to Nature's forces, including moonlight.
- Take a moment to honor your intentions. Keep watch over a few days as the sun, moon, wind, rain or snow, and heat or cold release their energy.
- When you feel your wishes are fully weathered, bring them indoors and safely burn the paper to release any remaining messages to the moon as you begin this new cycle of intentions.

What is your intention-setting focus today?

I am grateful for...

I am grateful for...

I am grateful for...

I am grateful for...

I am grateful for...

HOW DO YOU WANT TO FEEL TODAY?

IF YOU ARE JOURNALING IN THE MORNING, visualize your day going successfully and describe it here. **IF YOU ARE WRITING AT THE END OF THE DAY,** reflect on how the day went and write out how you would rescript any parts to be more successful.

DAY # 26 / /

What is your intention-setting focus today?

I am grateful for...

I am grateful for...

I am grateful for...

I am grateful for...

I am grateful for...

HOW DO YOU WANT TO FEEL TODAY?

IF YOU ARE JOURNALING IN THE MORNING, visualize your day going successfully and describe it here. **IF YOU ARE WRITING AT THE END OF THE DAY,** reflect on how the day went and write out how you would rescript any parts to be more successful.

DAY # 27 / /

What is your intention-setting focus today?

I am grateful for...

I am grateful for...

I am grateful for...

I am grateful for...

I am grateful for...

HOW DO YOU WANT TO FEEL TODAY?

IF YOU ARE JOURNALING IN THE MORNING, visualize your day going successfully and describe it here. **IF YOU ARE WRITING AT THE END OF THE DAY,** reflect on how the day went and write out how you would rescript any parts to be more successful.

DAY # 28 / /

What is your intention-setting focus today?

I am grateful for...

I am grateful for...

I am grateful for...

I am grateful for...

I am grateful for...

HOW DO YOU WANT TO FEEL TODAY?

IF YOU ARE JOURNALING IN THE MORNING, visualize your day going successfully and describe it here. **IF YOU ARE WRITING AT THE END OF THE DAY,** reflect on how the day went and write out how you would rescript any parts to be more successful.

DAY # 29 / /

What is your intention-setting focus today?

I am grateful for...

I am grateful for...

I am grateful for...

I am grateful for...

I am grateful for...

HOW DO YOU WANT TO FEEL TODAY?

IF YOU ARE JOURNALING IN THE MORNING, visualize your day going successfully and describe it here. **IF YOU ARE WRITING AT THE END OF THE DAY,** reflect on how the day went and write out how you would rescript any parts to be more successful.

DAY # 30 / /

What is your intention-setting focus today?

I am grateful for...

I am grateful for...

I am grateful for...

I am grateful for...

I am grateful for...

HOW DO YOU WANT TO FEEL TODAY?

IF YOU ARE JOURNALING IN THE MORNING, visualize your day going successfully and describe it here. **IF YOU ARE WRITING AT THE END OF THE DAY,** reflect on how the day went and write out how you would rescript any parts to be more successful.

DAY # 31 / /

What is your intention-setting focus today?

I am grateful for...

I am grateful for...

I am grateful for...

I am grateful for...

I am grateful for...

HOW DO YOU WANT TO FEEL TODAY?

IF YOU ARE JOURNALING IN THE MORNING, visualize your day going successfully and describe it here. **IF YOU ARE WRITING AT THE END OF THE DAY,** reflect on how the day went and write out how you would rescript any parts to be more successful.

DAY # 32 / /

What is your intention-setting focus today?

I am grateful for...

I am grateful for...

I am grateful for...

I am grateful for...

I am grateful for...

HOW DO YOU WANT TO FEEL TODAY?

IF YOU ARE JOURNALING IN THE MORNING, visualize your day going successfully and describe it here. **IF YOU ARE WRITING AT THE END OF THE DAY,** reflect on how the day went and write out how you would rescript any parts to be more successful.

Manifestation Statement for the Week

Action Plan

1.
2.
3.
4.
5.

	mon.	tues.	wed.	thu.	fri.	sat.	sun.
Daily Journaling							
Affirmations							
Gratitude							
369 Exercise							

Write your manifestation statement 3 times when you first wake up.

1.
2.
3.

MORNING

Take time during your day to write your manifestation statement 6 times.

1.
2.
3.
4.
5.
6.

DAY

Before you go to bed, write out your manifestation statement 9 times.

1.
2.
3.
4.
5.
6.
7.
8.
9.

NIGHT

MORNING

1.
2.
3.

DAY

1.
2.
3.
4.
5.
6.

NIGHT

1.
2.
3.
4.
5.
6.
7.
8.
9.

MORNING

1.
2.
3.

DAY

1.
2.
3.
4.
5.
6.

NIGHT

1.
2.
3.
4.
5.
6.
7.
8.
9.

Confronting Limiting Beliefs

A limiting belief is a belief or judgement you have about yourself that holds you back in some way.

Have you ever thought, I'm not good at that so I probably shouldn't even try? You're not alone. Everyone has some kind of negative belief about themselves and their abilities. But these judgements hold us back from growing and living out best lives.

Where do these beliefs come from? Some may have been taught to us when we were children, been inherited from our elders, or formed when we were teens or young adults. Limiting beliefs are defensive mechanisms that come from your brain's desire to protect you from perceived future pain.

Only through identifying and challenging these judgements can we move past them. **HERE ARE SOME EXAMPLES OF COMMON LIMITING BELIEFS:**

I'm not smart enough

I don't have the experience

Bad things happen to me

All my relationships are painful

I'm not talented enough

I don't deserve nice things

I'm not attractive

Other people's needs are more important than mine

WHAT IS A LIMITING BELIEF THAT IS HOLDING YOU BACK?

HOW DOES THIS BELIEF MAKE YOU FEEL?

THANK THIS BELIEF FOR HOW IT MAY HAVE PROTECTED YOU IN THE PAST.

Give yourself permission to move past this limiting beliefs.

I thank this belief for...

(ex. protecting me from possible disappointment.)

Time to flip the script! **CROSS OUT THE LIMITING BELIEF YOU WROTE ABOVE AND REWRITE THE BELIEF NOW COMING FROM A PLACE OF TRUTH, LOVE, AND EMPOWERMENT.**

What is your intention-setting focus today?

I am grateful for...

I am grateful for...

I am grateful for...

I am grateful for...

I am grateful for...

HOW DO YOU WANT TO FEEL TODAY?

IF YOU ARE JOURNALING IN THE MORNING, visualize your day going successfully and describe it here. **IF YOU ARE WRITING AT THE END OF THE DAY,** reflect on how the day went and write out how you would rescript any parts to be more successful.

DAY # 34 / /

What is your intention-setting focus today?

I am grateful for...

I am grateful for...

I am grateful for...

I am grateful for...

I am grateful for...

HOW DO YOU WANT TO FEEL TODAY?

IF YOU ARE JOURNALING IN THE MORNING, visualize your day going successfully and describe it here. **IF YOU ARE WRITING AT THE END OF THE DAY,** reflect on how the day went and write out how you would rescript any parts to be more successful.

DAY # 35 / /

What is your intention-setting focus today?

I am grateful for...

I am grateful for...

I am grateful for...

I am grateful for...

I am grateful for...

HOW DO YOU WANT TO FEEL TODAY?

IF YOU ARE JOURNALING IN THE MORNING, visualize your day going successfully and describe it here. **IF YOU ARE WRITING AT THE END OF THE DAY,** reflect on how the day went and write out how you would rescript any parts to be more successful.

DAY # 36 / /

What is your intention-setting focus today?

I am grateful for...

I am grateful for...

I am grateful for...

I am grateful for...

I am grateful for...

HOW DO YOU WANT TO FEEL TODAY?

IF YOU ARE JOURNALING IN THE MORNING, visualize your day going successfully and describe it here. **IF YOU ARE WRITING AT THE END OF THE DAY,** reflect on how the day went and write out how you would rescript any parts to be more successful.

DAY # 37 / /

What is your intention-setting focus today?

I am grateful for...

I am grateful for...

I am grateful for...

I am grateful for...

I am grateful for...

HOW DO YOU WANT TO FEEL TODAY?

IF YOU ARE JOURNALING IN THE MORNING, visualize your day going successfully and describe it here. **IF YOU ARE WRITING AT THE END OF THE DAY,** reflect on how the day went and write out how you would rescript any parts to be more successful.

DAY # 38 / /

What is your intention-setting focus today?

I am grateful for...

I am grateful for...

I am grateful for...

I am grateful for...

I am grateful for...

HOW DO YOU WANT TO FEEL TODAY?

IF YOU ARE JOURNALING IN THE MORNING, visualize your day going successfully and describe it here. **IF YOU ARE WRITING AT THE END OF THE DAY,** reflect on how the day went and write out how you would rescript any parts to be more successful.

What is your intention-setting focus today?

I am grateful for...

I am grateful for...

I am grateful for...

I am grateful for...

I am grateful for...

HOW DO YOU WANT TO FEEL TODAY?

IF YOU ARE JOURNALING IN THE MORNING, visualize your day going successfully and describe it here. **IF YOU ARE WRITING AT THE END OF THE DAY,** reflect on how the day went and write out how you would rescript any parts to be more successful.

What is your intention-setting focus today?

I am grateful for...

I am grateful for...

I am grateful for...

I am grateful for...

I am grateful for...

HOW DO YOU WANT TO FEEL TODAY?

IF YOU ARE JOURNALING IN THE MORNING, visualize your day going successfully and describe it here. **IF YOU ARE WRITING AT THE END OF THE DAY,** reflect on how the day went and write out how you would rescript any parts to be more successful.

Manifestation Statement for the Week

Action Plan

1.
2.
3.
4.
5.

✷	mon.	tues.	wed.	thu.	fri.	sat.	sun.
Daily Journaling							
Affirmations							
Gratitude							
369 Exercise							

369 *Method*

Write your manifestation statement 3 times when you first wake up.

1. ______________________
2. ______________________
3. ______________________

MORNING

Take time during your day to write your manifestation statement 6 times.

1. ______________________
2. ______________________
3. ______________________
4. ______________________
5. ______________________
6. ______________________

DAY

Before you go to bed, write out your manifestation statement 9 times.

1. ______________________
2. ______________________
3. ______________________
4. ______________________
5. ______________________
6. ______________________
7. ______________________
8. ______________________
9. ______________________

NIGHT

369 *Method*

MORNING

1.
2.
3.

DAY

1.
2.
3.
4.
5.
6.

NIGHT

1.
2.
3.
4.
5.
6.
7.
8.
9.

369 *Method*

MORNING

1.
2.
3.

DAY

1.
2.
3.
4.
5.
6.

NIGHT

1.
2.
3.
4.
5.
6.
7.
8.
9.

Letting Go of Negativity

To manifest positive change in your life, you need to let go of negative emotions like shame, anger, or resentment. These negative feelings drain your energy and prevent you from attracting positivity to your life. Use the following writing prompts to help you release

WHAT IS THE MOST NEGATIVE OR DIFFICULT THING/PERSON/IDEA THAT I NEED TO LET GO OF?

HOW WILL I FEEL ONCE I LET GO OF IT?

What is your intention-setting focus today?

I am grateful for...

I am grateful for...

I am grateful for...

I am grateful for...

I am grateful for...

HOW DO YOU WANT TO FEEL TODAY?

IF YOU ARE JOURNALING IN THE MORNING, visualize your day going successfully and describe it here. **IF YOU ARE WRITING AT THE END OF THE DAY,** reflect on how the day went and write out how you would rescript any parts to be more successful.

DAY # 42 / /

What is your intention-setting focus today?

I am grateful for...

I am grateful for...

I am grateful for...

I am grateful for...

I am grateful for...

HOW DO YOU WANT TO FEEL TODAY?

IF YOU ARE JOURNALING IN THE MORNING, visualize your day going successfully and describe it here. **IF YOU ARE WRITING AT THE END OF THE DAY,** reflect on how the day went and write out how you would rescript any parts to be more successful.

DAY # 43 / /

What is your intention-setting focus today?

I am grateful for...

I am grateful for...

I am grateful for...

I am grateful for...

I am grateful for...

HOW DO YOU WANT TO FEEL TODAY?

IF YOU ARE JOURNALING IN THE MORNING, visualize your day going successfully and describe it here. **IF YOU ARE WRITING AT THE END OF THE DAY,** reflect on how the day went and write out how you would rescript any parts to be more successful.

DAY # 44 / /

What is your intention-setting focus today?

I am grateful for...

I am grateful for...

I am grateful for...

I am grateful for...

I am grateful for...

HOW DO YOU WANT TO FEEL TODAY?

IF YOU ARE JOURNALING IN THE MORNING, visualize your day going successfully and describe it here. **IF YOU ARE WRITING AT THE END OF THE DAY,** reflect on how the day went and write out how you would rescript any parts to be more successful.

DAY # 45   /   /

What is your intention-setting focus today?

I am grateful for...

I am grateful for...

I am grateful for...

I am grateful for...

I am grateful for...

HOW DO YOU WANT TO FEEL TODAY?

IF YOU ARE JOURNALING IN THE MORNING, visualize your day going successfully and describe it here. **IF YOU ARE WRITING AT THE END OF THE DAY,** reflect on how the day went and write out how you would rescript any parts to be more successful.

What is your intention-setting focus today?

I am grateful for...

I am grateful for...

I am grateful for...

I am grateful for...

I am grateful for...

HOW DO YOU WANT TO FEEL TODAY?

IF YOU ARE JOURNALING IN THE MORNING, visualize your day going successfully and describe it here. **IF YOU ARE WRITING AT THE END OF THE DAY,** reflect on how the day went and write out how you would rescript any parts to be more successful.

DAY # 47 / /

What is your intention-setting focus today?

I am grateful for...

I am grateful for...

I am grateful for...

I am grateful for...

I am grateful for...

HOW DO YOU WANT TO FEEL TODAY?

IF YOU ARE JOURNALING IN THE MORNING, visualize your day going successfully and describe it here. **IF YOU ARE WRITING AT THE END OF THE DAY,** reflect on how the day went and write out how you would rescript any parts to be more successful.

Manifestation Statement for the Week

Action Plan

1.
2.
3.
4.
5.

✱	mon.	tues.	wed.	thu.	fri.	sat.	sun.
Daily Journaling							
Affirmations							
Gratitude							
369 Exercise							

Write your manifestation statement 3 times when you first wake up.

MORNING

1. ______
2. ______
3. ______

Take time during your day to write your manifestation statement 6 times.

DAY

1. ______
2. ______
3. ______
4. ______
5. ______
6. ______

Before you go to bed, write out your manifestation statement 9 times.

NIGHT

1. ______
2. ______
3. ______
4. ______
5. ______
6. ______
7. ______
8. ______
9. ______

MORNING

1.
2.
3.

DAY

1.
2.
3.
4.
5.
6.

NIGHT

1.
2.
3.
4.
5.
6.
7.
8.
9.

MORNING

1.
2.
3.

DAY

1.
2.
3.
4.
5.
6.

NIGHT

1.
2.
3.
4.
5.
6.
7.
8.
9.

Whom Do You Want to Be?

IN THIS VISUALIZATION EXERCISE, take time to imagine your future self. Fully imagining this person will help you begin to embody them. Who is this person? What do they value? *How do they present themselves to the world?*

What is your intention-setting focus today?

I am grateful for...

I am grateful for...

I am grateful for...

I am grateful for...

I am grateful for...

HOW DO YOU WANT TO FEEL TODAY?

IF YOU ARE JOURNALING IN THE MORNING, visualize your day going successfully and describe it here. **IF YOU ARE WRITING AT THE END OF THE DAY,** reflect on how the day went and write out how you would rescript any parts to be more successful.

DAY # 49 / /

What is your intention-setting focus today?

I am grateful for...

I am grateful for...

I am grateful for...

I am grateful for...

I am grateful for...

HOW DO YOU WANT TO FEEL TODAY?

IF YOU ARE JOURNALING IN THE MORNING, visualize your day going successfully and describe it here. **IF YOU ARE WRITING AT THE END OF THE DAY,** reflect on how the day went and write out how you would rescript any parts to be more successful.

DAY # 50 / /

What is your intention-setting focus today?

I am grateful for...

I am grateful for...

I am grateful for...

I am grateful for...

I am grateful for...

HOW DO YOU WANT TO FEEL TODAY?

IF YOU ARE JOURNALING IN THE MORNING, visualize your day going successfully and describe it here. **IF YOU ARE WRITING AT THE END OF THE DAY,** reflect on how the day went and write out how you would rescript any parts to be more successful.

DAY # 51 / /

What is your intention-setting focus today?

I am grateful for...

I am grateful for...

I am grateful for...

I am grateful for...

I am grateful for...

HOW DO YOU WANT TO FEEL TODAY?

IF YOU ARE JOURNALING IN THE MORNING, visualize your day going successfully and describe it here. **IF YOU ARE WRITING AT THE END OF THE DAY,** reflect on how the day went and write out how you would rescript any parts to be more successful.

DAY # 52 / /

What is your intention-setting focus today?

I am grateful for...

I am grateful for...

I am grateful for...

I am grateful for...

I am grateful for...

HOW DO YOU WANT TO FEEL TODAY?

IF YOU ARE JOURNALING IN THE MORNING, visualize your day going successfully and describe it here. **IF YOU ARE WRITING AT THE END OF THE DAY,** reflect on how the day went and write out how you would rescript any parts to be more successful.

DAY # 53 / /

What is your intention-setting focus today?

I am grateful for...

I am grateful for...

I am grateful for...

I am grateful for...

I am grateful for...

HOW DO YOU WANT TO FEEL TODAY?

IF YOU ARE JOURNALING IN THE MORNING, visualize your day going successfully and describe it here. **IF YOU ARE WRITING AT THE END OF THE DAY,** reflect on how the day went and write out how you would rescript any parts to be more successful.

DAY # 54 / /

What is your intention-setting focus today?

I am grateful for...

I am grateful for...

I am grateful for...

I am grateful for...

I am grateful for...

HOW DO YOU WANT TO FEEL TODAY?

IF YOU ARE JOURNALING IN THE MORNING, visualize your day going successfully and describe it here. **IF YOU ARE WRITING AT THE END OF THE DAY,** reflect on how the day went and write out how you would rescript any parts to be more successful.

Manifestation Statement for the Week

Action Plan

1.
2.
3.
4.
5.

✷	mon.	tues.	wed.	thu.	fri.	sat.	sun.
Daily Journaling							
Affirmations							
Gratitude							
369 Exercise							

Write your manifestation statement 3 times when you first wake up.

MORNING

1. __________
2. __________
3. __________

Take time during your day to write your manifestation statement 6 times.

DAY

1. __________
2. __________
3. __________
4. __________
5. __________
6. __________

Before you go to bed, write out your manifestation statement 9 times.

NIGHT

1. __________
2. __________
3. __________
4. __________
5. __________
6. __________
7. __________
8. __________
9. __________

MORNING

1.
2.
3.

DAY

1.
2.
3.
4.
5.
6.

NIGHT

1.
2.
3.
4.
5.
6.
7.
8.
9.

MORNING

1.
2.
3.

DAY

1.
2.
3.
4.
5.
6.

NIGHT

1.
2.
3.
4.
5.
6.
7.
8.
9.

Crystals for Manifestation

Crystals can be used to focus and harness the energy around and within us. The following crystals are especially helpful with manifestation.

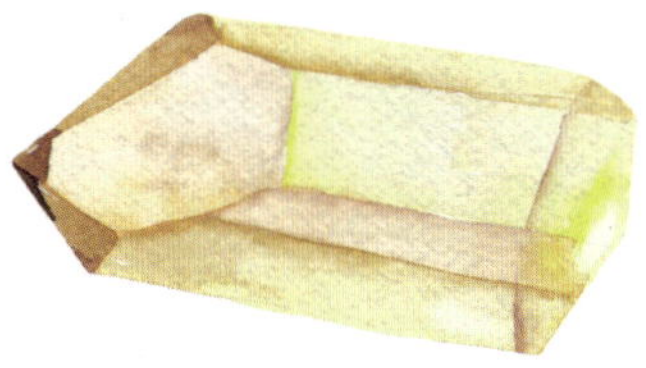

CITRINE

This joyous golden crystal is infused with optimism! It attracts prosperity of all kinds, financial or career success but more broadly realized as a happy, healthy, bountiful life. It is also known to boost self-confidence.

ROSE QUARTZ

Rose quartz is the stone of unconditional love—for yourself and others. So much of manifestation is about love and welcoming love into your life. This might be romantic love or self-love, compassion, and gratitude.

CLEAR QUARTZ

Clear quartz is known as "the master healer" and is a powerful crystal for health and healing. It also boosts all forms of manifestation and can be used in tandem with other crystals.

DAY # 55   /   /

What is your intention-setting focus today?

I am grateful for...

I am grateful for...

I am grateful for...

I am grateful for...

I am grateful for...

HOW DO YOU WANT TO FEEL TODAY?

IF YOU ARE JOURNALING IN THE MORNING, visualize your day going successfully and describe it here. **IF YOU ARE WRITING AT THE END OF THE DAY,** reflect on how the day went and write out how you would rescript any parts to be more successful.

What is your intention-setting focus today?

I am grateful for...

I am grateful for...

I am grateful for...

I am grateful for...

I am grateful for...

HOW DO YOU WANT TO FEEL TODAY?

IF YOU ARE JOURNALING IN THE MORNING, visualize your day going successfully and describe it here. **IF YOU ARE WRITING AT THE END OF THE DAY,** reflect on how the day went and write out how you would rescript any parts to be more successful.

What is your intention-setting focus today?

I am grateful for...

I am grateful for...

I am grateful for...

I am grateful for...

I am grateful for...

HOW DO YOU WANT TO FEEL TODAY?

IF YOU ARE JOURNALING IN THE MORNING, visualize your day going successfully and describe it here. **IF YOU ARE WRITING AT THE END OF THE DAY,** reflect on how the day went and write out how you would rescript any parts to be more successful.

DAY # 58 / /

What is your intention-setting focus today?

I am grateful for...

I am grateful for...

I am grateful for...

I am grateful for...

I am grateful for...

HOW DO YOU WANT TO FEEL TODAY?

IF YOU ARE JOURNALING IN THE MORNING, visualize your day going successfully and describe it here. **IF YOU ARE WRITING AT THE END OF THE DAY,** reflect on how the day went and write out how you would rescript any parts to be more successful.

DAY # 59 / /

What is your intention-setting focus today?

I am grateful for...

I am grateful for...

I am grateful for...

I am grateful for...

I am grateful for...

HOW DO YOU WANT TO FEEL TODAY?

IF YOU ARE JOURNALING IN THE MORNING, visualize your day going successfully and describe it here. **IF YOU ARE WRITING AT THE END OF THE DAY,** reflect on how the day went and write out how you would rescript any parts to be more successful.

What is your intention-setting focus today?

I am grateful for...

I am grateful for...

I am grateful for...

I am grateful for...

I am grateful for...

HOW DO YOU WANT TO FEEL TODAY?

IF YOU ARE JOURNALING IN THE MORNING, visualize your day going successfully and describe it here. **IF YOU ARE WRITING AT THE END OF THE DAY,** reflect on how the day went and write out how you would rescript any parts to be more successful.

DAY # 61 / /

What is your intention-setting focus today?

I am grateful for...

I am grateful for...

I am grateful for...

I am grateful for...

I am grateful for...

HOW DO YOU WANT TO FEEL TODAY?

IF YOU ARE JOURNALING IN THE MORNING, visualize your day going successfully and describe it here. **IF YOU ARE WRITING AT THE END OF THE DAY,** reflect on how the day went and write out how you would rescript any parts to be more successful.

DAY # 62 / /

What is your intention-setting focus today?

I am grateful for...

I am grateful for...

I am grateful for...

I am grateful for...

I am grateful for...

HOW DO YOU WANT TO FEEL TODAY?

IF YOU ARE JOURNALING IN THE MORNING, visualize your day going successfully and describe it here. **IF YOU ARE WRITING AT THE END OF THE DAY,** reflect on how the day went and write out how you would rescript any parts to be more successful.

Manifestation Statement for the Week

Action Plan

1.
2.
3.
4.
5.

✷	mon.	tues.	wed.	thu.	fri.	sat.	sun.
Daily Journaling							
Affirmations							
Gratitude							
369 Exercise							

369 Method

Write your manifestation statement 3 times when you first wake up.

MORNING

1. ___
2. ___
3. ___

Take time during your day to write your manifestation statement 6 times.

DAY

1. ___
2. ___
3. ___
4. ___
5. ___
6. ___

Before you go to bed, write out your manifestation statement 9 times.

NIGHT

1. ___
2. ___
3. ___
4. ___
5. ___
6. ___
7. ___
8. ___
9. ___

MORNING

1.
2.
3.

DAY

1.
2.
3.
4.
5.
6.

NIGHT

1.
2.
3.
4.
5.
6.
7.
8.
9.

MORNING

1.
2.
3.

DAY

1.
2.
3.
4.
5.
6.

NIGHT

1.
2.
3.
4.
5.
6.
7.
8.
9.

Whom Do You Admire?

LIST 3 PEOPLE YOU'VE ENCOUNTERED WHOM YOU ADMIRE. What is it about these individuals that attracts your attention and respect? Maybe they radiate positivity, joy, or compassion? Identifying and acknowledging these people can help you attract more similarly *positive people* into your life.

1. ______________________________

2. ______________________________

3. ______________________________

DAY # 63 / /

What is your intention-setting focus today?

I am grateful for...

I am grateful for...

I am grateful for...

I am grateful for...

I am grateful for...

HOW DO YOU WANT TO FEEL TODAY?

IF YOU ARE JOURNALING IN THE MORNING, visualize your day going successfully and describe it here. **IF YOU ARE WRITING AT THE END OF THE DAY,** reflect on how the day went and write out how you would rescript any parts to be more successful.

DAY # 64 / /

What is your intention-setting focus today?

I am grateful for...

I am grateful for...

I am grateful for...

I am grateful for...

I am grateful for...

HOW DO YOU WANT TO FEEL TODAY?

IF YOU ARE JOURNALING IN THE MORNING, visualize your day going successfully and describe it here. **IF YOU ARE WRITING AT THE END OF THE DAY,** reflect on how the day went and write out how you would rescript any parts to be more successful.

DAY # 65 / /

What is your intention-setting focus today?

I am grateful for...

I am grateful for...

I am grateful for...

I am grateful for...

I am grateful for...

HOW DO YOU WANT TO FEEL TODAY?

IF YOU ARE JOURNALING IN THE MORNING, visualize your day going successfully and describe it here. **IF YOU ARE WRITING AT THE END OF THE DAY,** reflect on how the day went and write out how you would rescript any parts to be more successful.

What is your intention-setting focus today?

I am grateful for...

I am grateful for...

I am grateful for...

I am grateful for...

I am grateful for...

HOW DO YOU WANT TO FEEL TODAY?

IF YOU ARE JOURNALING IN THE MORNING, visualize your day going successfully and describe it here. **IF YOU ARE WRITING AT THE END OF THE DAY,** reflect on how the day went and write out how you would rescript any parts to be more successful.

DAY # 67 / /

What is your intention-setting focus today?

I am grateful for...

I am grateful for...

I am grateful for...

I am grateful for...

I am grateful for...

HOW DO YOU WANT TO FEEL TODAY?

IF YOU ARE JOURNALING IN THE MORNING, visualize your day going successfully and describe it here. **IF YOU ARE WRITING AT THE END OF THE DAY,** reflect on how the day went and write out how you would rescript any parts to be more successful.

DAY # 68 / /

What is your intention-setting focus today?

I am grateful for...

I am grateful for...

I am grateful for...

I am grateful for...

I am grateful for...

HOW DO YOU WANT TO FEEL TODAY?

IF YOU ARE JOURNALING IN THE MORNING, visualize your day going successfully and describe it here. **IF YOU ARE WRITING AT THE END OF THE DAY,** reflect on how the day went and write out how you would rescript any parts to be more successful.

What is your intention-setting focus today?

I am grateful for...

I am grateful for...

I am grateful for...

I am grateful for...

I am grateful for...

HOW DO YOU WANT TO FEEL TODAY?

IF YOU ARE JOURNALING IN THE MORNING, visualize your day going successfully and describe it here. **IF YOU ARE WRITING AT THE END OF THE DAY,** reflect on how the day went and write out how you would rescript any parts to be more successful.

Manifestation Statement for the Week

Action Plan

1.
2.
3.
4.
5.

✷	mon.	tues.	wed.	thu.	fri.	sat.	sun.
Daily Journaling							
Affirmations							
Gratitude							
369 Exercise							

Write your manifestation statement 3 times when you first wake up.

1.
2.
3.

MORNING

Take time during your day to write your manifestation statement 6 times.

1.
2.
3.
4.
5.
6.

DAY

Before you go to bed, write out your manifestation statement 9 times.

1.
2.
3.
4.
5.
6.
7.
8.
9.

NIGHT

MORNING

1.
2.
3.

DAY

1.
2.
3.
4.
5.
6.

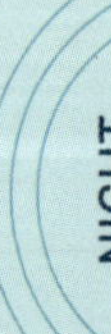

NIGHT

1.
2.
3.
4.
5.
6.
7.
8.
9.

MORNING

1.
2.
3.

DAY

1.
2.
3.
4.
5.
6.

NIGHT

1.
2.
3.
4.
5.
6.
7.
8.
9.

You Have So Much to Offer

LIST 5 *gifts* THAT YOU BRING TO THE WORLD.

1.

2.

3.

4.

5.

DAY # 70 / /

What is your intention-setting focus today?

I am grateful for...

I am grateful for...

I am grateful for...

I am grateful for...

I am grateful for...

HOW DO YOU WANT TO FEEL TODAY?

IF YOU ARE JOURNALING IN THE MORNING, visualize your day going successfully and describe it here. **IF YOU ARE WRITING AT THE END OF THE DAY,** reflect on how the day went and write out how you would rescript any parts to be more successful.

What is your intention-setting focus today?

I am grateful for...

I am grateful for...

I am grateful for...

I am grateful for...

I am grateful for...

HOW DO YOU WANT TO FEEL TODAY?

IF YOU ARE JOURNALING IN THE MORNING, visualize your day going successfully and describe it here. **IF YOU ARE WRITING AT THE END OF THE DAY,** reflect on how the day went and write out how you would rescript any parts to be more successful.

DAY # 72 / /

What is your intention-setting focus today?

I am grateful for...

I am grateful for...

I am grateful for...

I am grateful for...

I am grateful for...

HOW DO YOU WANT TO FEEL TODAY?

IF YOU ARE JOURNALING IN THE MORNING, visualize your day going successfully and describe it here. **IF YOU ARE WRITING AT THE END OF THE DAY,** reflect on how the day went and write out how you would rescript any parts to be more successful.

What is your intention-setting focus today?

I am grateful for...

I am grateful for...

I am grateful for...

I am grateful for...

I am grateful for...

HOW DO YOU WANT TO FEEL TODAY?

IF YOU ARE JOURNALING IN THE MORNING, visualize your day going successfully and describe it here. **IF YOU ARE WRITING AT THE END OF THE DAY,** reflect on how the day went and write out how you would rescript any parts to be more successful.

What is your intention-setting focus today?

I am grateful for...

I am grateful for...

I am grateful for...

I am grateful for...

I am grateful for...

HOW DO YOU WANT TO FEEL TODAY?

IF YOU ARE JOURNALING IN THE MORNING, visualize your day going successfully and describe it here. **IF YOU ARE WRITING AT THE END OF THE DAY,** reflect on how the day went and write out how you would rescript any parts to be more successful.

DAY # 75 / /

What is your intention-setting focus today?

I am grateful for...

I am grateful for...

I am grateful for...

I am grateful for...

I am grateful for...

HOW DO YOU WANT TO FEEL TODAY?

IF YOU ARE JOURNALING IN THE MORNING, visualize your day going successfully and describe it here. **IF YOU ARE WRITING AT THE END OF THE DAY,** reflect on how the day went and write out how you would rescript any parts to be more successful.

What is your intention-setting focus today?

I am grateful for...

I am grateful for...

I am grateful for...

I am grateful for...

I am grateful for...

HOW DO YOU WANT TO FEEL TODAY?

IF YOU ARE JOURNALING IN THE MORNING, visualize your day going successfully and describe it here. **IF YOU ARE WRITING AT THE END OF THE DAY,** reflect on how the day went and write out how you would rescript any parts to be more successful.

Manifestation Statement for the Week

Action Plan

1.
2.
3.
4.
5.

	mon.	tues.	wed.	thu.	fri.	sat.	sun.
Daily Journaling							
Affirmations							
Gratitude							
369 Exercise							

Write your manifestation statement 3 times when you first wake up.

1.
2.
3.

MORNING

Take time during your day to write your manifestation statement 6 times.

1.
2.
3.
4.
5.
6.

DAY

Before you go to bed, write out your manifestation statement 9 times.

1.
2.
3.
4.
5.
6.
7.
8.
9.

NIGHT

MORNING

1.
2.
3.

DAY

1.
2.
3.
4.
5.
6.

NIGHT

1.
2.
3.
4.
5.
6.
7.
8.
9.

MORNING

1.
2.
3.

DAY

1.
2.
3.
4.
5.
6.

NIGHT

1.
2.
3.
4.
5.
6.
7.
8.
9.

Surprise!

Take time to recognize and savor surprises. You have manifested these "surprises." **USE THIS SPACE TO RECORD UNEXPECTED, *surprising* EVENTS AND EXPRESS YOUR GRATITUDE FOR THEM.**

DAY # 77 / /

What is your intention-setting focus today?

I am grateful for...

I am grateful for...

I am grateful for...

I am grateful for...

I am grateful for...

HOW DO YOU WANT TO FEEL TODAY?

IF YOU ARE JOURNALING IN THE MORNING, visualize your day going successfully and describe it here. **IF YOU ARE WRITING AT THE END OF THE DAY,** reflect on how the day went and write out how you would rescript any parts to be more successful.

DAY # 78 / /

What is your intention-setting focus today?

I am grateful for...

I am grateful for...

I am grateful for...

I am grateful for...

I am grateful for...

HOW DO YOU WANT TO FEEL TODAY?

IF YOU ARE JOURNALING IN THE MORNING, visualize your day going successfully and describe it here. **IF YOU ARE WRITING AT THE END OF THE DAY,** reflect on how the day went and write out how you would rescript any parts to be more successful.

DAY # 79 / /

What is your intention-setting focus today?

I am grateful for...

I am grateful for...

I am grateful for...

I am grateful for...

I am grateful for...

HOW DO YOU WANT TO FEEL TODAY?

IF YOU ARE JOURNALING IN THE MORNING, visualize your day going successfully and describe it here. **IF YOU ARE WRITING AT THE END OF THE DAY,** reflect on how the day went and write out how you would rescript any parts to be more successful.

What is your intention-setting focus today?

I am grateful for...

I am grateful for...

I am grateful for...

I am grateful for...

I am grateful for...

HOW DO YOU WANT TO FEEL TODAY?

IF YOU ARE JOURNALING IN THE MORNING, visualize your day going successfully and describe it here. **IF YOU ARE WRITING AT THE END OF THE DAY,** reflect on how the day went and write out how you would rescript any parts to be more successful.

What is your intention-setting focus today?

I am grateful for...

I am grateful for...

I am grateful for...

I am grateful for...

I am grateful for...

HOW DO YOU WANT TO FEEL TODAY?

IF YOU ARE JOURNALING IN THE MORNING, visualize your day going successfully and describe it here. **IF YOU ARE WRITING AT THE END OF THE DAY,** reflect on how the day went and write out how you would rescript any parts to be more successful.

What is your intention-setting focus today?

I am grateful for...

I am grateful for...

I am grateful for...

I am grateful for...

I am grateful for...

HOW DO YOU WANT TO FEEL TODAY?

IF YOU ARE JOURNALING IN THE MORNING, visualize your day going successfully and describe it here. **IF YOU ARE WRITING AT THE END OF THE DAY,** reflect on how the day went and write out how you would rescript any parts to be more successful.

DAY # 83 / /

What is your intention-setting focus today?

I am grateful for...

I am grateful for...

I am grateful for...

I am grateful for...

I am grateful for...

HOW DO YOU WANT TO FEEL TODAY?

IF YOU ARE JOURNALING IN THE MORNING, visualize your day going successfully and describe it here. **IF YOU ARE WRITING AT THE END OF THE DAY,** reflect on how the day went and write out how you would rescript any parts to be more successful.

Manifestation Statement for the Week

Action Plan

1.
2.
3.
4.
5.

✱	mon.	tues.	wed.	thu.	fri.	sat.	sun.
Daily Journaling							
Affirmations							
Gratitude							
369 Exercise							

369 *Method*

Write your manifestation statement 3 times when you first wake up.

MORNING

1.
2.
3.

Take time during your day to write your manifestation statement 6 times.

DAY

1.
2.
3.
4.
5.
6.

Before you go to bed, write out your manifestation statement 9 times.

NIGHT

1.
2.
3.
4.
5.
6.
7.
8.
9.

1.
2.
3.

DAY

1.
2.
3.
4.
5.
6.

NIGHT

1.
2.
3.
4.
5.
6.
7.
8.
9.

MORNING

1.
2.
3.

DAY

1.
2.
3.
4.
5.
6.

NIGHT

1.
2.
3.
4.
5.
6.
7.
8.
9.

Good Vibes

What sort of energy do you give out to others?

DAY # 84 / /

What is your intention-setting focus today?

I am grateful for...

I am grateful for...

I am grateful for...

I am grateful for...

I am grateful for...

HOW DO YOU WANT TO FEEL TODAY?

IF YOU ARE JOURNALING IN THE MORNING, visualize your day going successfully and describe it here. **IF YOU ARE WRITING AT THE END OF THE DAY,** reflect on how the day went and write out how you would rescript any parts to be more successful.

What is your intention-setting focus today?

I am grateful for...

I am grateful for...

I am grateful for...

I am grateful for...

I am grateful for...

HOW DO YOU WANT TO FEEL TODAY?

IF YOU ARE JOURNALING IN THE MORNING, visualize your day going successfully and describe it here. **IF YOU ARE WRITING AT THE END OF THE DAY,** reflect on how the day went and write out how you would rescript any parts to be more successful.

DAY # 86 / /

What is your intention-setting focus today?

I am grateful for...

I am grateful for...

I am grateful for...

I am grateful for...

I am grateful for...

HOW DO YOU WANT TO FEEL TODAY?

IF YOU ARE JOURNALING IN THE MORNING, visualize your day going successfully and describe it here. **IF YOU ARE WRITING AT THE END OF THE DAY,** reflect on how the day went and write out how you would rescript any parts to be more successful.

DAY # 87 / /

What is your intention-setting focus today?

I am grateful for...

I am grateful for...

I am grateful for...

I am grateful for...

I am grateful for...

HOW DO YOU WANT TO FEEL TODAY?

IF YOU ARE JOURNALING IN THE MORNING, visualize your day going successfully and describe it here. **IF YOU ARE WRITING AT THE END OF THE DAY,** reflect on how the day went and write out how you would rescript any parts to be more successful.

DAY # 88 / /

What is your intention-setting focus today?

I am grateful for...

I am grateful for...

I am grateful for...

I am grateful for...

I am grateful for...

HOW DO YOU WANT TO FEEL TODAY?

IF YOU ARE JOURNALING IN THE MORNING, visualize your day going successfully and describe it here. **IF YOU ARE WRITING AT THE END OF THE DAY,** reflect on how the day went and write out how you would rescript any parts to be more successful.

DAY # 89 / /

What is your intention-setting focus today?

I am grateful for...

I am grateful for...

I am grateful for...

I am grateful for...

I am grateful for...

HOW DO YOU WANT TO FEEL TODAY?

IF YOU ARE JOURNALING IN THE MORNING, visualize your day going successfully and describe it here. **IF YOU ARE WRITING AT THE END OF THE DAY,** reflect on how the day went and write out how you would rescript any parts to be more successful.

DAY # 90 / /

What is your intention-setting focus today?

I am grateful for...

I am grateful for...

I am grateful for...

I am grateful for...

I am grateful for...

HOW DO YOU WANT TO FEEL TODAY?

IF YOU ARE JOURNALING IN THE MORNING, visualize your day going successfully and describe it here. **IF YOU ARE WRITING AT THE END OF THE DAY,** reflect on how the day went and write out how you would rescript any parts to be more successful.

Manifestation Statement for the Week

Action Plan

1.
2.
3.
4.
5.

✷	mon.	tues.	wed.	thu.	fri.	sat.	sun.
Daily Journaling							
Affirmations							
Gratitude							
369 Exercise							

Reflections

As you begin the final stretch of 100 days of manifestation, take a minute to reflect on this journey.

HOW HAS YOUR LIFE CHANGED?

HOW HAS YOUR MINDSET CHANGED?

WHAT CONTINUES TO POSE A STRUGGLE?

DAY # 91 / /

What is your intention-setting focus today?

I am grateful for...

I am grateful for...

I am grateful for...

I am grateful for...

I am grateful for...

HOW DO YOU WANT TO FEEL TODAY?

IF YOU ARE JOURNALING IN THE MORNING, visualize your day going successfully and describe it here. **IF YOU ARE WRITING AT THE END OF THE DAY,** reflect on how the day went and write out how you would rescript any parts to be more successful.

What is your intention-setting focus today?

I am grateful for...

I am grateful for...

I am grateful for...

I am grateful for...

I am grateful for...

HOW DO YOU WANT TO FEEL TODAY?

IF YOU ARE JOURNALING IN THE MORNING, visualize your day going successfully and describe it here. **IF YOU ARE WRITING AT THE END OF THE DAY,** reflect on how the day went and write out how you would rescript any parts to be more successful.

DAY # 93 / /

What is your intention-setting focus today?

I am grateful for...

I am grateful for...

I am grateful for...

I am grateful for...

I am grateful for...

HOW DO YOU WANT TO FEEL TODAY?

IF YOU ARE JOURNALING IN THE MORNING, visualize your day going successfully and describe it here. **IF YOU ARE WRITING AT THE END OF THE DAY,** reflect on how the day went and write out how you would rescript any parts to be more successful.

What is your intention-setting focus today?

I am grateful for...

I am grateful for...

I am grateful for...

I am grateful for...

I am grateful for...

HOW DO YOU WANT TO FEEL TODAY?

IF YOU ARE JOURNALING IN THE MORNING, visualize your day going successfully and describe it here. **IF YOU ARE WRITING AT THE END OF THE DAY,** reflect on how the day went and write out how you would rescript any parts to be more successful.

DAY # 95 / /

What is your intention-setting focus today?

I am grateful for...

I am grateful for...

I am grateful for...

I am grateful for...

I am grateful for...

HOW DO YOU WANT TO FEEL TODAY?

IF YOU ARE JOURNALING IN THE MORNING, visualize your day going successfully and describe it here. **IF YOU ARE WRITING AT THE END OF THE DAY,** reflect on how the day went and write out how you would rescript any parts to be more successful.

What is your intention-setting focus today?

I am grateful for...

I am grateful for...

I am grateful for...

I am grateful for...

I am grateful for...

HOW DO YOU WANT TO FEEL TODAY?

IF YOU ARE JOURNALING IN THE MORNING, visualize your day going successfully and describe it here. **IF YOU ARE WRITING AT THE END OF THE DAY,** reflect on how the day went and write out how you would rescript any parts to be more successful.

DAY # 97 / /

What is your intention-setting focus today?

I am grateful for...

I am grateful for...

I am grateful for...

I am grateful for...

I am grateful for...

HOW DO YOU WANT TO FEEL TODAY?

IF YOU ARE JOURNALING IN THE MORNING, visualize your day going successfully and describe it here. **IF YOU ARE WRITING AT THE END OF THE DAY,** reflect on how the day went and write out how you would rescript any parts to be more successful.

DAY # 98 / /

What is your intention-setting focus today?

I am grateful for...

I am grateful for...

I am grateful for...

I am grateful for...

I am grateful for...

HOW DO YOU WANT TO FEEL TODAY?

IF YOU ARE JOURNALING IN THE MORNING, visualize your day going successfully and describe it here. **IF YOU ARE WRITING AT THE END OF THE DAY,** reflect on how the day went and write out how you would rescript any parts to be more successful.

What is your intention-setting focus today?

I am grateful for...

I am grateful for...

I am grateful for...

I am grateful for...

I am grateful for...

HOW DO YOU WANT TO FEEL TODAY?

IF YOU ARE JOURNALING IN THE MORNING, visualize your day going successfully and describe it here. **IF YOU ARE WRITING AT THE END OF THE DAY,** reflect on how the day went and write out how you would rescript any parts to be more successful.

DAY # 100 / /

What is your intention-setting focus today?

I am grateful for...

I am grateful for...

I am grateful for...

I am grateful for...

I am grateful for...

HOW DO YOU WANT TO FEEL TODAY?

IF YOU ARE JOURNALING IN THE MORNING, visualize your day going successfully and describe it here. **IF YOU ARE WRITING AT THE END OF THE DAY,** reflect on how the day went and write out how you would rescript any parts to be more successful.

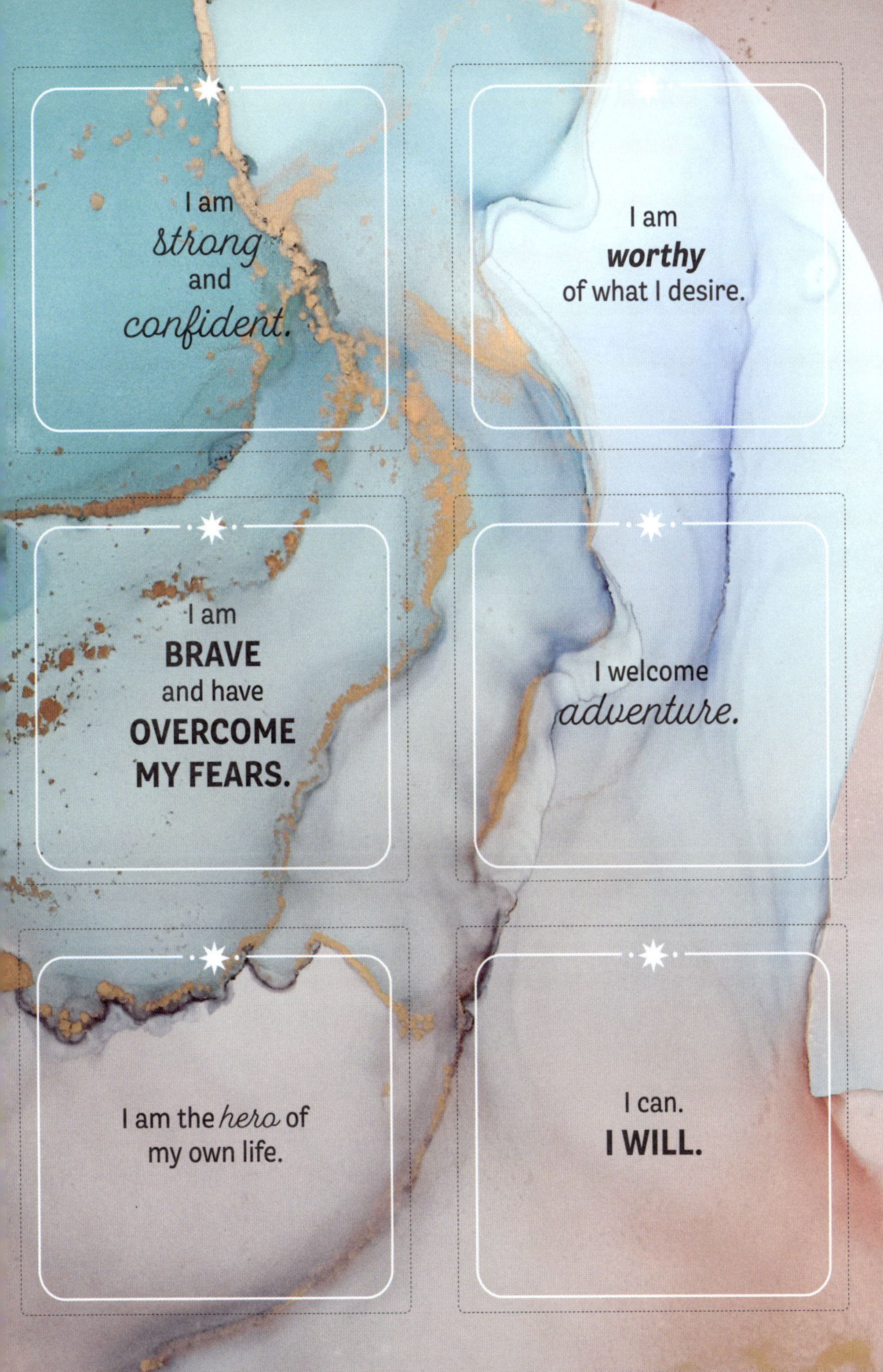
I am *strong* and *confident.*
I am **worthy** of what I desire.
I am **BRAVE** and have **OVERCOME MY FEARS.**
I welcome *adventure.*
I am the *hero* of my own life.
I can. **I WILL.**

Everyday is a
fresh start.

I am
wealthy
beyond money.

I am
MAKING TODAY COUNT.

IT'S MY TIME.

My life is
rich and full.

I am allowed to have
success
and
happiness.

I am *worthy* of love.
I am *radiating love.*
I believe in my **SKILLS** and **TALENTS.**
Wherever I go, I find *love.*
I am attracting a ***genuine connection.***
I TRUST the process.